Men Who G
Men's

Most of my life I allowed people to see 80 percent of who I really was, including my wife. I was terrified that if people knew all of me, they'd have the ability to fully reject me. Group gave me a safe place to air my junk—all of it—and still feel unconditional love. It gave me the courage to face some of my greatest fears, like confessing everything to my wife. Little did I know that being 100 percent transparent was the key to a level of intimacy with my wife and close friends that I had never experienced before. I can honestly say that my group has been the catalyst to the freedom, empowerment, and life I experience today.
Josh, 31

When I first joined group I couldn't feel anything. Within this last year I gave all that I had to group. I remember the moment when I realized I wasn't just sober, but free. I was crying hard, driving home alone and I kept repeating the phrase, "I never thought I would be healthy." Life is a lot better when you can experience both pain and love at the same time. Group saved a lot more than just my life.
Cody, 21

Since attending men's purity group, my life has changed. I was living life knowing I'm a son of God, but never believing I could actually attain the freedom that a son has. I went to group to get help with my porn problem, but I received so much more. I found connection with my heart, understanding my needs, the safety of vulnerability, and a much stronger connection with my wife. My life will NEVER be the same again!
Gabe, 24

When I started coming to group I couldn't conceive of not looking at porn. I had been trapped in it my whole life. Now I have been free, really free, from porn and lust for eight years. James 5:16 confession and healing is my ongoing reality in my group. My former lust toward women is now gone because my need for comfort and acceptance that I formally met through porn has been met by a deep intimacy with Holy Spirit, my wife, and the men in my small group. This is who I was made to be. I am so grateful.
Phil, 50

When I came to this group I was addicted to drugs, alcohol, and porn. On top of that I was hiding it all from my wife and lying to her about it on a daily basis. Guilt and shame had completely stripped me of my confidence and authority. While going to group I rapidly developed a dangerously vulnerable relationship with three men who helped me learn through practice how to have a completely honest and transparent relationship with myself and my wife. I have established a new standard of transparency and intimacy with my wife. My future is no longer dictated by my past and I have learned to love myself. My wife feels safe for the first time in her life. My kids are glowing with life and love. My whole family is now walking confidently in authority and value for themselves. Oh yeah, and I don't look at porn, or do any kind of drugs, and no longer abuse alcohol.
Randy, 26

I had always thought that I would struggle with my purity, that my job was to fight the good fight. When I came to group I realized that I had to open myself up and let my walls down in order for God to truly heal me from the inside out. My surrender not only led to my freedom but a revival of my heart.
Josh, 38

I came to men's group because my struggle with lust had obliterated my second marriage. The pain it inflicted on my ex-wife, my kids, and me, had me in a desperate place. I joined a small group, and in a little less than three years I have learned to love myself, express my needs, manage emotional pain, the value of vulnerability, found my true masculine heart, and formed deep bonds with guys that I know will stand by me and not reject me. I have been promoted three times at work, doubled my income, work less hours, and now travel less for work. I was recently in Las Vegas for an entire week for work at a trade show and was able to overcome lust to the point of seeing nudity at every turn and not having to look away to maintain a pure heart.
Dave, 44

GET NAKED

A MAN'S GUIDE TO GREAT SEX

MARK PETERSON

Artzaintsa Books

Artzaintsa Books
www.Artzaintsa.com

Copyright © 2013 by Mark Peterson
All rights reserved.

PRINTED IN THE UNITED STATES OF AMERICA
17 16 15 14 13   1 2 3

ISBN: 978-0-98984-831-2

Scripture taken from the HOLY BIBLE, NEW INTERNATIONAL VERSION ®. Copyright © 1973, 1978, 1984 by International Bible Society. Used by permission of Zondervan Publishing House. All rights reserved.

Cover design: Artzaintsa Books & By the Stream Media
Interior design: Artzaintsa Books

Publisher's Cataloging-in-Publication Data
Peterson, Mark.
Get naked: a man's guide to great sex/Mark Peterson.
ISBN 978-0-98984-831-2 (pbk)
ISBN 978-0-98984-833-6 (ebk)
1. Sex—Religious aspects—Christianity. 2. Christian men—Conduct of life. I. Title.
BT708.P48 2013
241'.66 P48
2013949997

CONTENTS

9
PART 1: GETTING NAKED
How to get your penis under control.

27
PART 2: SMALL GROUP IS A BIG DEAL
How to start and lead a small group.

47
PART 3: GO BIG
How to run and grow a men's sexual purity group in your church.

79
FIVE SMOOTH STONES
Important subjects for further reading.

A NOTE FROM MARK

This is a book for men. It's short on purpose. Most everything included here I've learned the hard way through the experience of sitting alongside other men in small groups and doing life with them. I have had great mentors and friends (both male and female), as well as many mighty men to sow into over the past twenty years, of which I am grateful. May your life be as relationally full as mine has and may you learn a little easier than I did. I wrote *Get Naked* in hopes that you do.

In this book, when I refer to "my group," or "our group," I am referring to the men's sexual purity group at my church. I started the group in 2007 with just a few other men. I did it for me. I could impress you with our attendance numbers, but I don't want to count the fighting men. The success of the group continues to rest on the commitment of the men in the room and the love they have for each other.

There are thirteen brief stories scattered throughout the book about men whose lives have been changed. No one's name has been changed to protect anyone.

1
GETTING NAKED

THIS BOOK WAS WRITTEN FOR YOU. IT'S ABOUT SEXUAL PURITY, the foundation that you build the rest of your life on. To get everything you really want in life, you have got to get this right first. It's the deepest place you go. It's the core of who you are. It's where you were created, and it mirrors your worship with the living God.

To get sexually pure you must get naked. You must become known and let others see who you are. Adam and Eve were in the garden naked and not ashamed. They sinned, hid, and covered themselves up, but Jesus died naked on a cross so that we can live naked and not ashamed.

Purity is the prerequisite to great sex. You can have a lot of sex, but you will never have great sex outside of sexual purity, because without purity the only thing that can be satisfied is your carnal man. Great sex is hard work and it will cost you. The price is purity. To get there you will need to be honest. Dangerously honest. No religion involved.

The message in this book is not about controlling your behavior. It's about being sexually free from the inside out, not just sexually sober.[1] I define sexual freedom as the ability to be in a room full of naked Brazilian models and have eyes for only your wife.

If you're single, purity and all that comes with it is preparation for marriage. Prepare well, as you will get what you are. The woman you choose to marry will be different from you in many ways, but she'll be your equal when it comes to your level of personal health. If a man is not sexually pure, marriage does not help get his penis under control; it only makes it worse. It is much easier to work on you when you are still single, so use this time purposefully, because when you're ready, she'll be there. You will find everything you want in a wife when you are everything you know you should be. Purity precedes great sex.

If you're in bad shape right now, know that on your journey to

---

1. "Sober" in this book is defined as not acting out sexually.

holiness it often gets worse before it gets better. What took you ten years to get into isn't going to take two weeks to get out of. It takes time, hard work, discipline, and pain. When you stop whatever stupid thing you were doing, you will feel pain. Pain was there all along, but it was masked by sexual sin, your leading choice of pain management.

If you're screwed up, you are not alone. In my experience (and the stats back me), about 65 percent of men in the church and 85 percent out of the church are looking at porn and masturbating weekly, among other more devastating choices of sexual sin.[2] The elephant is in the room and he is so fat you can't see anyone. If you want to get better your hope lies in the transforming power of Jesus Christ. If you are not a believer now is your chance. Repeat after me and say it out loud.

> *Jesus, forgive me of my sins.*
> *Come into my life and change me from the inside out.*
> *Don't let me go.*
> *Show me what it is to know you.*
> *Help me to follow you wholeheartedly all the days of my life.*
> *Amen.*

You men that are Christians and didn't pray, know that you are about to experience a second conversion similar to your first. You will fall in love with Jesus all over again through radical honesty and deep relationship. He will unlock the deeper mysteries of who he is and allow you to see life with a totally different perspective. Though having to walk through the consequences of sexual sin would not be my first choice for anyone, a man who has been sexually redeemed is a powerful person. He has no choice but to be. It's a violent battle out. Victory goes to him who is all in, where there is no option but to win. When you dig down deep and you're honest and desperate, the God you have only read about in the Bible will fully come alive to you, his presence felt, his love tangible.

---

2. "Pornography Research," Josh McDowell Ministry, accessed September 20, 2013, https://s3.amazonaws.com/jmm.us.j1ca/Pornography+Research+-+ALL.pdf.

PART ONE GETTING NAKED

Jesus said if a man lusts after a woman in his heart he has as good as slept with her.[3] For generations of men in Christendom that sentence has been burdensome. It begs the question, "How can I ever live up to that?" The dominant feeling is despair. The good news is that it wasn't meant to be condemning, it was meant to set that standard of freedom. He wants you free from sexual sin from the inside out, not a whitewashed tomb full of dead men's bones; he is doing the dishes and washing the inside of the cup.[4]

Here is the highlight reel of what you already know. Scripture makes it clear to run from sexual sin and Joseph modeled that.[5] We are to let there not be even a hint of sexual immorality.[6] All excellent directives. Yet, he wants all of us right down to the core so that there is no lust in the heart. Getting to that place doesn't involve running. Running is a great choice in a place of weakness, but if you want the whole enchilada, to be holy as he is holy, that comes with you taking a stand.[7]

That really hot twenty-year-old you saw downtown today wasn't the devil trying to tempt you. That was the Holy Spirit trying to heal you. Instead of rebuking your thoughts or trying real hard not to look, recognize what is going on. Let a dicey situation give you insight into what you really need. The things that attracted you to her will show you what you need. If it was her breasts, you need comfort or nurture. If it was her butt, legs, or belly button, then you need acceptance.[8] The point is that whatever is pulling on you puts a magnifying glass on a legitimate need. Your job is to go get your real need met in a healthy way. If you don't find what brings you life, what brings death will find you.

Porn is an empty and destructive way of meeting your need for adventure, beauty, discovery, danger, or significance. Once you recognize what you need, transfer that energy to a healthy event.

---

3. Matthew 5:28.
4. Matthew 23:26–27.
5. 1 Corinthians 6:18; Genesis 39.
6. Ephesians 5:3.
7. 1 Peter 1:15–16.
8. Russell Willingham, *Breaking Free: Understanding Sexual Addiction & the Healing Power of Jesus.* (Illinois: InterVarsity Press, 1999), 168–173.

Go on a road trip, cliff diving, hunting, fishing, bungee jumping, skydiving, go to a football game with friends, or climb a mountain. No man will summit a peak over 10,000 feet and beat off. It will never happen. He's fully alive in a dangerous situation filled with the beauty of creation. His God-given need is met.

Learning to recognize the need and getting it met in a healthy way gets you out of the cycle of addiction. If you get triggered by something and call a friend to get some prayer, that's a great move. Keep it up. However, the very fact that you're getting triggered shows that you are not taking care of yourself and you have work to do. Get to know you. Learn what your heart needs and go climb that mountain before you see the hot twenty-year-old and you won't give her a second look.

Jesus is the model for purity. Though a man, he was tempted

When Casey first came to group he was looking at porn and suffering the consequences that come with it. Kyle, his group leader, told him right off to share something in group each week that he had never told anyone before. Kyle also reinforced to him that the most vulnerable guys get better the fastest. Casey believed him, and week after week he laid his stuff out on the table. Every week the other men in the group met his confessions with love, acceptance, and understanding. He began to heal from the inside out.

After several months in group, he said to his wife, "From this moment on, you will be my only source of sexual gratification." He repented for the harm his sexual sin had done to their marriage and family. Their sex life dramatically improved along with their communication and friendship. They are in love and have a great marriage.

His wife is a rock star as well. We had her in to speak at group last year and she killed it. His children are in great shape too, which is beautiful to see. He continues to push into broken parts of his life courageously and help other men get better. He is a frequent speaker, posts blogs on our website regularly, and is one of the best small group leaders in the room.

in every way.⁹ At the moment when he was weak, tired, hungry, and lonely, the devil took him up on the mountain and rolled out the IMAX screen, giving him a fantastic visual, and offered him entire professional cheerleading squads all at once. Jesus said, "No thanks, I'm good. I know who I am, who my Father is, and what I am called to do."¹⁰

He looked temptation in the eye and stared it down. Like the bronze snake in the desert; God said to look at it and live.¹¹ The very thing that was killing God's people was what they needed to look at to get better. Ignoring the problem or pretending it's not there is not faith. It's denial. Look at it and live.

HONESTY

> (Jenny) "You ever want to be somebody Forrest?"
>
> (Forrest) "Aren't I just supposed to be me?"
>
> ***Forrest Gump***

To look at it and live is to be honest. It's easier to live up to the seventh commandment of not committing adultery when we are obeying the ninth and telling the truth.¹² Ephesians 4:25 says, "Put off falsehood and speak truthfully to your neighbor." Most people don't speak the truth because of fear of rejection. If they tell someone who they really are, there is a chance that they can be completely rejected—and that's scary. Most can't handle that, so they play it safe by living in a world where lies of self-protection are commonplace. People have gotten so far from truth-telling that they start sentences by saying, "to be honest," in order to brace one another for the truth.

Honesty is the doorway to your freedom. Through it you will find everything you have been looking for. If we walk in the light

---

* A paraphrased version of the script, *Forrest Gump*, Robert Zemekies, 1994.
9. Hebrews 4:15.
10. Matthew 4:8–11; Luke 4:5–8.
11. Numbers 21:4–9.
12. Exodus 20:14, 16.

as he is in the light we have true fellowship with each other.[13] That, gentlemen, is metaphorically getting naked and becoming known. It gives us the ability to make true friends that know us and love us for who we really are. When we do that, we receive the full promise of 1 John 1:7, and the blood of Jesus, his son, purifies us from all sin. That's good news.

When we talk about what is really going on inside, it's like flipping on a light switch in the basement; it lets us see what is down there. Opening up gets the junk out and what we need in. We are starved for real relationship. The only way to get the kind of relationships that go down deep and start healing your heart is to let people in and let them know who you really are, what you love, what you would rather do without, what you struggle with, what is imperfect in your life. We don't want to live two layers deep in the nine-layer bean dip. There is more for us. We want to scrape the bottom of the dish and enjoy the whole thing.

We're as sick as the secrets we keep. The question shouldn't be, "Who do I have to tell?" Rather it should be, "Who shouldn't I tell?" A good way to tell if you're getting better is to ask yourself if you are the same person everywhere you go? If the answer is yes, you're doing it right.

Start practicing honesty by journaling. Don't hide behind religious buzzwords. When you use them you don't have to think about what you're saying. Dig deeper. Be real. Push past the familiar, superficial, churchy expressions and use your own vocabulary to explain yourself. Write in such a way that if your notebook was ever found you would be ruined. David is an excellent example of getting his heart out on paper. Just read though the Psalms to see how it's done. David had problems just like you that he needed God to solve. Honesty in writing and in relationships, coupled with abandonment in worship produced solutions in his life. He says in Psalms 32:3, "When I kept silent, my bones wasted away." Lay it all out on the table, men. Confession gives us access to the power of the cross.

We're only as honest as we feel safe, so find safe people. Understand

---

13. 1 John 1:7.

> Andy is from England; he came to the group sober but far from free inside. A man with a stout build, Andy struggles with his weight; overeating was his masturbation and he is winning that fight. He had been successful in a religious sense, but was bleeding on the inside with a heart full of unmet needs he could no longer ignore. He was deeply impacted by the honesty of the group. I would often catch him listening in on my conversations with other men in the room. With an expression of shock, he would blush many different shades of red, followed by euphoric giggling. His eyes kept telling me he had found a home in the room, where honesty is our highest value.
>
> Andy took what I gave him, improved it, and made it his own. He is probably the most dangerously honest man I know. He is kind-hearted and a phenomenal leader. I love him because he embarrasses me with the level of vulnerability on the things that come out of his mouth, and not many people can do that for me. Sometimes when he is speaking I want to crawl under my chair. Honesty made him a powerful man.
>
> Today he is one of our regular speakers. He has the ability to tell great stories out of his own life, relate to other men, and teach what he has learned. He doesn't care about being popular, but he is one of the most popular men in the room. He is also one of our best small group leaders. He is a counselor and meets with men from the group regularly. Many owe a large part of their freedom to him. He has built excellent relationships, and he is finding what his heart needs and is going after it in a healthy way. I remember him saying from the pulpit once, "This group saved my life." And he has helped to save ours too.

that everyone has an intimacy level they can handle. On a scale of one to ten, ten being the most transparent, recognize where others are and meet them there. Only be as honest as other people can handle. You might push them a point or two higher on a rare occasion, but if you dial it up too high, you'll lose them. On the flip side, find some dangerously honest people that scare you. They'll be the ones that push you to go deeper. I have a lot of the former and a few of the latter. We need both. Maintain a healthy balance and take it for what it is—a big fat adventure into the unknown of self-discovery.

RELATIONSHIPS

When you're ready to be honest, you're ready for relationship. Sexual sin is a selfish act that hurts others and will isolate you. The more you do it, the further away you get from what you really need. Learn to make and maintain healthy friendships. Become the friend you want to have. Care, ask questions, and really listen to the answers. These are simple acts of selflessness that will pay you back. Do the relational work before you are in crisis so when the trials do come, you're ready with relational change in the bank.

David is the Old Testament model for sexual purity.[14] You know the story. Despite the mess he created with his affair for both his family and his country, he finished well. In fact, he was the only king in biblical history to give away his throne before his death.

David finished well because he had friends. Samson, who also yielded to sexual temptation, was blinded, mocked, and committed suicide, dying in chains.[15] Though equal in combat prowess and prophetic destiny, the difference between the two was friends. David had them, Samson did not.

The relational structure of David should be aspired to. He had fathers in Jesse, Samuel, and Nathan and peers in Jonathan, Joab, Bathsheba, and Abigail. He also had his mighty men; they protected him, encouraged him, defended him, and told him when he was wrong. They saved his life and helped make David great. When you add mothers to the list of fathers, peers, and mighty men, together these relationships form your own personal phalanx formation. Build that kind of relational structure around yourself and greatness awaits you too.

---

14. 1 Samuel 16–1 Kings 2:12; 1 Chronicles 10–1 Chronicles 29:30.
15. Judges 13–16.

> Paul is one of my favorite guys because he's just flat-out raw. If he ever gets up to do a testimony everybody in the room is going to feel it. He models honesty better than anyone I know. When he came to group, he had already come out of a gay lifestyle but was still struggling with homosexual desires, porn, and masturbation. Being introverted, his tendencies were to hide his deep brokenness, but he courageously chose against it, and has ever-so-slowly continued to dig deeper into pure relational intimacy with other men and his God. His honesty and vulnerability has been the cornerstone of his healing.
>
> Since being at group, he met a wonderful woman whom he married. They just had a son last year which has been a huge healing component for him in itself. He is an occasional speaker and leads a great small group. When you're with Paul you feel loved. He's a good man and there is extra grace on his life to give grace to others.

Make Friends

Relationships hurt us, and it's relationships that will heal us. Sexual addiction is a relational and intimacy disorder. Ironically, we have to push into the very thing that scares us the most in order to be healed: relationship. Face the fear, say no to the isolation that wants to kill you, and make friends. Friends = freedom.

When choosing friends, Jesus is the model. The first thing he did right after he came out of an intense time of temptation was figure out who he was going to be in relationship with and what it was going to look like; it's an example of the most powerful use of the prophetic gifting—determining who should be in your life and how. He tapped Peter, Andrew, James, John, and others.[16] He went from temptation to relationship. He spent time with them. They were his closest friends and confidants. He sowed into them and they changed the world. Time = discipleship.

Be intentional about your friendships. The locationships that

---

16. Matthew 4:18–22.

come with school, work, or sports are not enough. Our heart needs friendships that are pure and not mired in politics, the marketplace, or competition. You have to work at relationship. Call, return calls, hang out, stay up with the current events in your friends' lives. Know what's going on with their work, marriage, and kids. Learn what your friends' dreams are and help them achieve them. Do things they like to do. I like football, but if a friend wants to watch the Stanley Cup, I'm there. I like it because he likes it and I like him. I like steak, but if he is raving about some new Thai place, yeah, let's try it.

Be there for the hard times; do what you can to help. When friends are in crisis, they are usually a little numb and can't think very clearly. Take pass on saying, "If you need anything, let me know." Few respond to this vague offer for help. Rather, get in your friends' lives and figure out what they do need, then jump in and help them.

Pay attention to who is on your mind. If someone keeps floating through your mind and then starts to hang out in your thoughts, that's the Holy Spirit trying to connect you. Give them a call. You'll be surprised at how many times they'll say, "No way! I was just thinking about you."

The best way to make friends is to find men that are in transition: men who have just moved, have become unemployed, are switching jobs, starting a business, or having a child. The uncertainty and trauma of life's big events open men up to relationship. Most men are really busy and transition in life opens up windows of availability to build a friendship. Find these guys and push in. Encourage them, help them in a tough time, and you'll make a long-term friend.

Friendships change over time. Don't be sad when a friend moves away. Many pull away, but this is a time you can push in. Bless them, help them, and encourage them. When friends move, it's an opportunity to articulate how you feel about them like no other time. To keep these friends, you must keep in touch. I have friends all around the country and a few internationally that I regularly call a few times a year for no other reason than to catch up and maintain the friendship. You can't grow a friendship very well outside of close geography, but you can maintain it. Don't let these friends slip away. You have history together that only time can build. It's work, but it will pay you back. I always tell my buddies that it helps if they move somewhere cool so I can visit and eat their food. God loves me because my friends live in great places like Southern California, Texas, Washington, British Columbia, Florida, and Montana. Now I just need a few of them to move to Wyoming, France, Israel, Italy, and the UK.

Be Available

To do relationship well you have to be available. Without availability the best you can have is locationships, and that's empty. I made a t-shirt once that said, "My friends answer the phone." The point is that they are available—that's why we're friends.

My favorite word is no. No gives me the ability to say yes. The more I say no to good things, the more I can say yes to great things. I work really hard not to make appointments or live on a set schedule. When I book something, it's usually last-minute, since I want to have an open schedule as long as I can. The most desirable thing about being self-employed is the freedom to schedule your own life. You will work harder, but it's on your own terms. Availability = relationship.

Accountability Doesn't Work

I don't like the word accountability and neither do you. Someone mouthed that word at Promise Keepers twenty years ago and it's been preached like it's the gospel ever since. Accountability is not in the Bible, and it doesn't work. I hear terms and phrases like "accountability group" or "I need you to keep me accountable" all the time. Absolutely not. I won't do it, and I categorically reject the word in that sense. Accountability wants to be a policeman, and I refuse.

Men hide behind accountability all the time, it shifts the weight of responsibility off the man who should carry it, and onto the man who shouldn't. What men want, what men need, is relationship not accountability.

Forgiveness Frees You

Forgiveness is for you. Unforgiveness keeps you in your own personal prison. If you're going to have healthy relationships that get you better, then you're going to have to learn to forgive. People will let you down and we have to be able to let it go. Life is a big experiment in failure. Being right doesn't help you in relationship. Being wrong and owning it does. If you have wronged someone, go and make it right. Use the words, "I'm really sorry I did that, will you forgive me?" If your actions caused someone financial loss, make amends with your checkbook as well as your

---

Blair came to group stuck in religious purgatory. After coming to Christ he was bored. He missed the girls and the beer. He had managed through some form of religious discipline to keep his clothes on with the women, but he was looking at porn and sexually amped up all the time. It took him getting mad at what religion had made him into to finally say, "No, I am not going to live that way anymore."

Like every man's story, his started with being honest, then bringing out more honesty. Positive things started to happen in his life when he finally had a knock-down, drag-out fight with God in his garage. He's been on a rocket ship ever since, pulling as many guys as he can along for the ride.

I watched him get sick of his job, quit, start his own business, go broke, and work off the debt with a manual labor job in the Midwest. He then started another business where he is finding success and loves to go to work.

Blair tried to step down from being a small group leader at least three times that I can think of because of a sexual failure. I was able to talk him out of it each time. One time I told him, "You can quit when I tell you you can quit." I'm so glad he listened to me. Today he is probably one of the best non-married small group leaders we have ever had, and his men love him.

He is really good at helping men get through hard stuff a little easier than he did. He is also a really good speaker who I am confident will, in time, be great. Watch for him.

words. When we work through something hard that affected a relationship and come out good on the other side, it only deepens the friendship.

When we pray for those who have hurt us we're not giving them a pass. We're asking that the living God do a mighty transformational work in their lives. These things hurt in all the right ways, just as God's transforming work in your own life is painful to get you where you need to be. We can't chase everybody down and fix every relationship because we only have control of our side of things, but we can forgive. Forgiveness frees you up to love deeply. It's a supernatural event that takes place on the inside and is preceded by our choice to let go. Forgiveness = friendship.

Find the Right Source

God uses relationships to heal us, but even the best relationships don't outweigh our relational need for God. Sometimes it's easier to make a call than to pray. Jesus is your source. He is our healer, our provider, our father. When we try to find what we need from men that only he can provide, we come up empty. Learn to distinguish what type of relationship you need at different times in your life—that of your friends, or intimacy with your God.

I recently went through a very dark spiritual time. If I had to rate it (I like to rate everything) it would have been the second hardest time spiritually for me in the last twenty years. I went to a lot of counseling, sometimes twice a week. I was mad, sad, and hurting. A large majority of my closest friends didn't even know what I was going through. They knew I was hurting, but I didn't tell most of them all the details and for the ones I did tell, I kept it brief. I knew they couldn't help me and I didn't want to pull them down or cash in any of my relational change. What I needed and what I got, I could only get from heaven.

So it is with all our relationships. Not only do we have to know what we need; we have to discern what others need as we're interacting with them so we can point them to the source if they aren't meant to get what they need from us. If we don't make the right call, trying to help them can feel like getting pulled under by a drowning man, and we end up wasting time and energy, and losing relational equity, not gaining it. No amount of personal relationship can help some people at certain times in life, it has to come from God. He has what we need.

Use the Tools

Being honest and building relationships are the two non-negotiable tools that you must use to get sexually pure. The following list will also help you, but know that tools only buy you time. Each one has its place. Use them; they keep you from doing something stupid. In the end we need Jesus to heal us. But to free us from the desire for dumb while we wait for him to finish what he's started, we need the tools.[17] They position us for an encounter with the living God, and that's where we are healed. These are the basic blocking and tackling drills that win games. I like trick plays as much as anyone, but they only work when the fundamentals of the game are done right. Train yourself and use them well.

TOOLS THAT BUILD THE HOUSE OF HOLINESS

1. **Get in a group.** This is covered in the next section of the book in detail, and I spend a forth of the book on the dynamics of small group because it's important, very important. This is a team sport, not an individual event. We need each other.

2. **Worship.** Worship is warfare. It is anything that brings intimacy with God. Worshipers get well because worship fills your heart with what you were created to hold.

3. **Call someone.** When you call when you're in trouble, you win. The call gets you in the light and breaks that isolation; it's a reminder that you are not alone.[18] It's an act of humility that says, "I need help. Can you pray for me?"

4. **Get rid of anything that is dragging you down.** Internet, smart phone, negative relationships, video games, alcohol, TV, social media, movies, even geographical areas. You may even need to switch jobs. When we purge the unhealthy and unnecessary

---

17. Philippians 1:6.
18. 1 John 1:7.

from our lives it makes room for the good that God wants to do. Nothing on the list needs to be avoided permanently, only for a time as you establish purity.

5. **Eat right.** Fuel your body with real food made from scratch. Get away from as many processed foods as you can. Go heavy on the fruits and vegetables, and eat organic as often as you can. When you eat good, you feel good, and you do good.

6. **Rest.** Failures happen when we are tired. Patton said, "Fatigue makes cowards of us all." I take a nap almost everyday. I get some grief for it from people, but it's a game changer for me. Take comfort that great men often nap. Stonewall Jackson and Napoleon would take naps during pitched battles. Churchill napped an hour a day even during the bombings of London. Naps give you the best of both worlds, you can stay up late and get up early, and as long as you take a nap, you're good.

7. **Disciplines.** There's a great book on this that any man who wants to get his penis under control should read called *Celebration of Discipline* by Richard Foster. It covers the disciplines of prayer, meditation, study, fasting, simplicity, solitude, and service.

8. **Activity.** Our bodies need to move. If you're not into working out at a gym, choose to do chores, sports, swimming, physical labor, or the hiking that goes with hunting or fishing. It feels good to get the blood pumping. It gets our heads clear so we can make good decisions.

9. **Work.** Men need to work; it's who we are. It's amazing what a few months of hard manual labor will do for the soul. When you get paid, pay your bills on time and stay out of debt. Live simply: less is more, stress is less. Work hard, play hard, rest easy.

10. **Counseling.** Sometimes we need a pro to help us look in places we wouldn't have gotten to on our own. Find good counselors by referral. Good counseling deals with the origin of the problem and brings healing to that place. It digs into the past and gets you current with today.

There are not just ten "tools to handle your tool," there are hundreds, but these are some of the main tools that will be a huge help in getting sexually sober. The most important thing they do for you is position you for a touch from the Lord that brings deep healing so that you are not just sexually sober but inwardly free. Tools hold you down and let Jesus heal you. An encounter from God in our lives keeps us from being the guy who brings a knife to a gun fight, it levels the playing field. No matter how good we get at being honest, building relationships, or using the tools, it's God's presence that transforms lives from the inside out. Time and again, God has met me when I'm at the end of me with waves of supernaturally felt love, acceptance, and divine circumstances. We have what we need to be holy as he is holy because he has made a home inside of us.

There are many more tools, some of which will be covered in the next section about small groups. Many others you will learn for yourself the hard way and by watching the lives of other men in the group you join. In your small group you'll have a front row seat at a life lecture on what works and what doesn't. Time and experience will be your favorite professor.

2
SMALL GROUP IS A BIG DEAL

I CAN'T SAY ENOUGH, GENTLEMEN, ABOUT HOW IMPORTANT A SMALL GROUP IS.
If you had to choose one thing to do to get better, choose to be in a small group. If there's not already a small group that you can join at your church, then you'll have to start one because you need it for you. Not only that, the men at your church need you to start a group. The need is huge and the opportunity is great.

Starting this group is a noble task worthy of your greatest effort. It's a smart move that will pay you back—not just you, but your family, church, and community as well, and not just today or next month, but for the years and decades to come through the lives of men you sow into.

In small group, we work on the whole man, not just his penis. Guys come to group for a carburetor adjustment and end up getting a full engine rebuild. The cool part about a group where the starting point is what a man does with his penis, is that it addresses the very most important thing in a man's life. There is no deeper place you can go than your sexuality, so the intimacy in the group is unparalleled.

Helping men get better is a high call that you will love. They need help, we have the answers, and the best part is that you'll get better too. You were created to lead and this group will draw out your greatness. Some men fail, but most grow like summer corn.

You won't be able to fake it; the others in your group will smell that a mile away. You will have to gut yourself regularly. If you don't, you will lead in title only, because the most vulnerable man in the room is the most powerful man in the room. Men follow courage, not titles. Be courageous.

This section is a combat leader's field guide on how to lead a small group. It will help you get men sexually pure and free, not just sober. Do the group for you. If it's not good for you, it's not good for anyone. It is impossible to love your neighbor as yourself if you don't love you.[1]

It's your assignment to get these men clean. You can the do the one-step, the twelve-step, or the Texas Two-Step; it doesn't matter to me how you go about it, just that you get it done. You will be surprised by your ingenuity, and in time you will add to this Wikipedia of mastery in leading men to sexual purity. Your true long-term success will be determined not in how many men you lead to freedom, but how many group leaders you create along the way.

If you think this is an addiction and accountability ministry, you have it all wrong. I have a strong dislike for all three of those words, and if you want to get men free and not just sober, you will too. What works and what we do in a small group is completely relationship based. Relationships hurt you, and the irony is that it's relationships that will heal you. Men are lonely because they have been hurt and relationships are dangerous and scary. A man will speed climb the Eiger and risk his life but die lonely. To get better you have to do danger. To get others better you must model it.

MY JOB (AND YOUR JOB) IS NOT DONE UNTIL:
You are having the best sex of your life.
You have an enviable marriage.
You have friendships that others want.

---

1. Leviticus 19:18; Mark 12:31.

STARTING YOUR GROUP

First, get the blessing of your pastor. Keep it low-key. Say something along the lines of, "Hey pastor Bob, I want to start a men's sexual purity group in our church. I am just going to start with a few men and see how it goes. Will you bless me?" Get prayed up and go for it. The response you get will be positive because your pastor has been praying for you to step forward and do it. The church has a problem, and the men's group you are about to start is the solution.

Next, find some men (at least two and no more than six—that's seven including you). It won't be too hard because the vast majority of the men in your church are struggling sexually. Use your prophetic gifting to identify who to invite. Be purposeful about it, as each one of those men will be your future leaders (See Part 3).

Don't advertise or promote the group. A changed life is your promotion. Good restaurants don't need an advertising campaign. You want to stay undercover for as long as you can. Let the fruit of changed lives speak for itself.

In your group, you'll talk about what went on during the week and any major events that might have stirred up some issues. You'll talk about your successes, your failures, what you're scared of, what hurts, what you want to do, what you're not doing, and all the whys behind this stuff. You're letting men get to know you and giving them a window into your life, and they're doing the same. As the men in your group communicate all this, you can see where they are and what they need. The group leader models how to do this, and asks questions to draw the men out and get them talking.

Break the paradigm of "another program" (because this isn't a program) and meet together outside of the group. Eat together; help each other outside of the room. Be men together; have fun.

Lead Like You

Your group should look like you and not like anyone else. Copy someone only long enough to find who you are, then run with it. Your men need you a lot more than they need a formula or a program. I have yet to see a man be a great group leader his first year. If you are about to start leading, I hope you will be the first. In

> Eli came to group mired in some of the worst religious denial I have ever seen and in a marriage that barely had a heartbeat. The group offended every part of who he was, but he was desperate because he couldn't reconcile his convictions with his lifestyle of porn and masturbation, so he committed to coming to the group every week. Slowly he dug himself out of the hole by being as honest as he knew how to be each week in small group and he started to get better.
>
> After being in the group for over a year, he got tired of the way he was living his life and the shallowness of his marriage. So he went home with nothing to lose and told his wife everything. They had it out until the sun came up. This was the turning point that brought him back to life. Today he is one of the most honest men in the room and is taking huge leaps forward in his own personal health. He has built healthy friendships and is an excellent small group leader. The change in his marriage is one of the most dramatic I have ever seen. You can tell how good they're doing by looking into the eyes of his wife. He and his wife are fully alive, connected, and in love. They are starting a food service business in town that I am confident will be successful. He just told me, "I love working with my wife." It's been an awfully hard go for him, but God has been faithful to meet him every step of the way and it's been beautiful to watch. He spoke at group a few months ago. I wasn't there but heard from everyone that he was the best speaker we had all summer.

your second year you're pretty good. Your third year you're great, and on your fourth year you can teach it. The point? It takes time.

You all may not have been mentored perfectly, if you were, there would be no need to read this book. The information here will help a bit, but the short of it is that you just need to crawl down in the trenches and get a shot at it, make mistakes, and see what works and what doesn't. The biggest thing is commitment. The most committed leaders are the best leaders. Be there every week, listen, love, pray, and encourage, and your men will transform over time right before your eyes. It's pretty cool.

The South had great generals; it liked them religious and a bit mad. After you have built trust, be a little crazy; your men will love you for it. Patton rightly said, "I have never had a great commander who is not a prima donna."

One Rule

We only have one rule in small group and that is confidentiality. Nothing leaves the room. If your pastor asks about someone specifically, respond by saying, "Sorry, I am bound by the confidentiality of the group." This makes it safe for a man to say what he needs to say to get better.[2]

You're going to hear some things that will be hard to listen to in your small group. Avoid judging other men by understanding and focusing on what is going on with them on the inside, not on the act itself. Religion wants to judge outward actions. There are reasons why men in your group do what they do, find the reasons and let go of whatever dumb thing they did and give them grace. God forgives us through the act of confession. Many men have trouble receiving forgiveness, so let your response to their screwups be a reaction that frees them from shame and guilt. It's easier not to be mad at or judge a man when you understand his past. So get history and keep focused on the inside of the man.

---

2. Confidentiality doesn't cover situations where the law is being broken. Your pastoral oversight should be notified in cases that are in question.

Not being judged is a gift that you want too. Feeling judgment from others when we're risking being honest is a real bummer, but we have to care more about getting better than we care about what other people think of us.

THESE ARE NOT RULES BUT STRONG SUGGESTIONS:
- No cross-talking or interrupting.
- Pray vertically, not horizontally.
- No church words.
- Show up every week unless you are out of town or hospitalized.

Group Size

Seven men is max group size—a leader and six guys works best. If you have eight men in a group and everybody shows up, split the group in half (with the healthiest guy in the group leading for the night) so each man can have more time to talk. The leader needs to be there a minimum of three out of four weeks, four out of five is better. If you are there more than that, miss one on purpose and take your wife on a date so another guy in the group can get a chance to lead without you.

Treat Every Man the Same

Sit in a circle, not an oval, or worse, at a rectangular table with you at the head. The circle says, "We are in this together. There is nothing between us, and I am on equal ground with you." It's like Jesus *feng shui*. If a guy is talking only to me because I'm the leader, I say something like, "I'm not the only guy in the group. They are going to help you as much as I am, so talk to them too." Just keep putting back on the group anything they want to put on you.

Many men (it's about 20 percent for us) are coming to the group because they struggle with same-sex attraction. Treat every man the same; there is nothing special that needs to be done. Love them, hug them, treat them like a man. On average, we have one guy in each small group who is struggling with homosexuality. What's really cool is that they get in a group with six other guys who have heterosexual struggles. Over time everyone in the group comes to understand that it's the same pain, it's just manifested differently. It's healing for everyone in the group. It's deeply satisfying to watch the process of men finding acceptance, love, and understanding. Over time these guys begin to

---

After Drew had been in group for about six months, we were doing a really cool, once a year thing called "breaking vows." Instead of going through the exercise, when his turn came, he stood up in front of everyone and said, "I feel like I have been lying to you guys. I have never told anyone this, but I have been struggling with homosexual desires my entire life. I just had to say it. I've been holding it in for too long." There was a moment of shock, and then he got a long standing ovation from everyone in the room, followed by hug after hug of acceptance.

There was a look of huge relief on his face, followed shortly afterward by the terror of what he had done. It was so bad that I would not have been surprised one bit had I gotten a call that he had jumped off a bridge. He stayed in that place for the next three weeks. He kept coming to group, but it was a dark place for him, real dark. Then God met him and he had a massive encounter with the love of Jesus. He was all smiles and couldn't stop laughing when he talked. In the middle of his sentences he would start to giggle, then laugh for no apparent reason, and he stayed in that place for over a year.

Since that time he went from being a partly employed painter to making his living from his art and loving it. He has fully come alive and not just in his vocational passions; he is also seriously dating a fantastic woman whom we hope he will marry. As I write this today, he is leaving for Montana where he will be teaching at a newly founded school of art.

date, get married, have kids, and build a family. It's a beautiful thing to be a part of.

Nice Doesn't Work

It has to be okay with you if guys leave. Either drive them into the group or out of it. Allow no middle ground. You don't want them to leave, but until you bring them to that place of decision, they can't get better. You are their friend when you say the hard things, and you have to be okay if you never see them again.

You cannot gently pastor men into getting better—nice doesn't work. If you love these guys, you can kick them in the nuts and they will thank you for it later.

That all sounded a little rough, but that is where you need to live. Again, you cannot lovingly pastor men into getting better (new leaders try this all the time and fail). I give guys about six weeks of nice. That month and a half of grace gives them some time to settle in, build trust, and for us to get some relational history. At that point, if a guy is stuck, I start to turn up the heat with tough questions that get him out of no-man's-land.

I just watched about five seasons of *Biggest Loser* with my family. There are two trainers, Bob and Jillian. Jillian is tough, yet compassionate with her clients. She gets in their heads, they cry, they get mad at her, but she gets results, and they love her in the end. Bob is great. Everybody loves Bob and wants to have him as a trainer. However after six seasons against Jillian, only one of Bob's people has won the title. It has been enjoyable to watch Bob get tougher over time. He actually started yelling at people. I love it. He stopped putting up with their crap. He stopped rescuing and he started to win.

Time

Managing your group time is a huge factor. If you respect it, the men will respect you; plus you'll get a lot more done by limiting the time, not just letting it run you. I like to lay out hard and fast rules on group time before we start each week with the goal of when we will be done. It usually goes something like this: I look at the clock. It's 8:15 and I want to be done by 9:15. I do the math. I have seven guys, so let's take six minutes each so that we'll have about twenty minutes to pray for each other at the end. I pull out a phone and use the stopwatch to time each man. When he is getting close to the end of his time and it doesn't feel like he is wrapping up, I will give him a thirty-second warning. If it's deep and he is really getting somewhere, I might say something like, "You can have one of my minutes." This doesn't cut him off, but it puts pressure to wrap it up because he is taking from the group leader's time and that is valuable.

Limiting the time each person gets to talk does a bunch of stuff for you:

- It keeps the diarrhea mouths from running on and on, which ruins men's groups around the globe (a universal time limit, described above, would solve the problem).
- It draws out the men who don't know how to talk. At first they will only say a few things with little meaning because they have never been listened to before and don't know what to do with it. Let them sit in the quiet. Honor them with the group's time. Ask them a question to keep them going. I have seen many a man's man cry over this as they try to speak because someone finally cared enough to listen and to value them. It's glorious.
- It helps men learn to articulate themselves quickly and precisely. This is the most important benefit of watching the clock; it's huge because guys need to learn this to get better and stay better.

The guys in your group are learning to get a lot said in a short amount of time. When this is learned, it goes so much better for them because no one outside of the group is going to let them ramble on for five minutes unless it's a paid shrink. On the outside you will get thirty seconds, not five minutes, and this is practice.

A good homework assignment is to get men to practice what

they are going to talk about in the mirror at home before they show up so it flows. This will pay them back down the road in every part of life.

Leave time to pray and prophesy over each other at the end of each group. (If you are an evangelical, all that means is encouragement and to give them hope for the future so they don't jump off a bridge.) If a man can see his future he can get through his crap. Find God's heart for your men and you will fall in love with them. I can't tell you how many times I have started a new group and thought, "Man, these guys are jacked up. I don't even like anyone in here," only to later on love each one deeply.

Hug

Most men didn't get the physical affection they needed growing up so they end up violating their values to meet a need. Their father didn't do it, so make up for lost time and touch your men a lot. Hug each time before you leave and hold on a second longer than is comfortable. The number one love language for men is touch (the Christian way of saying "sex"), and touch meets a huge need, so do it, and do it regularly. The cool part about hugging is that you get one too.

Their Healing Is Not Your Responsibility

For most of these men, getting better is just showing up, connecting with other men, and airing out their junk in a place they won't be judged for it. The only real accountability we do is that we expect each man to tell us how he did sexually at the beginning of his time to talk each week. This way we know where he is right away. Knowing he'll have to tell us all how he did with his penis this week right away, helps a guy to fight it. Nobody wants to show up and have the first thing out of his mouth be that he did something stupid.

You can't police a man to sobriety; if you do, it won't last. It's a good thing that policing has no long-term value because it's way too much work. Let the men do the work, and don't work

> Jason dropped out of group three times. When he came back his fourth time I put him in my small group under the condition that he would not miss one group for any reason. If he did, he would be out of our small group. He agreed.
>
> When he got to the point in time when he usually quit group (about four months in) he hit a wall. I saw him do it, he was stuck. Through counseling, and courageously digging through the junkyard of his past, using the tools, and keeping his commitment, he got through the wall.
>
> Today he is doing great, sexually and in the marketplace with his work. He took over my small group and has become a really good leader, worthy to be followed. He has a gift and the patience to work with other men that get stuck. I like to hear him talk, he is always digging deeper into his heart and inviting Jesus into the places that hurt.

on their problems more than they do. Yes, there is some peer pressure in the small group, but it works only to a point. They have to want it for themselves. The outward discipline of say, not looking at porn, draws out the internal pain that pushed a man to it in the first place.

When your men are in pain, it's good, that's what you want. Pain is your friend. It lets you know you're alive. Pain is the place that God heals. If you're feeling pain, you're doing it right. It's what they have been trying to avoid, and now that they're in pain you have something to work with because a desperate man in pain is teachable. When a man controls his behavior, it sets him up for the good things God wants to do.

Be Courageously Honest

The men in your group are learning how to talk, they are learning how to feel, and so are you. Get naked and be as honest as you know how to be; we are all learning and when you do it, the men in your group will follow you. When Napoleon returned from Elba Island he said, "Strike me down or follow me." His troops followed.

Just keep encouraging your men to be as honest as they can. Be patient, because their "honest as they can" this week will be significantly more honest two months from now. The onion gets peeled down slowly. What's going on in the male mind during this process is the line of thinking that says, "If they knew the real me they wouldn't love me. If they reject me, then I am truly rejected at my core, so I will show them my false self." See the cycle? It's what got them in the room in the first place. So stand up and clap when they say something courageously honest. They will love you for it.

Down and dirty, real, brutal honesty is their only hope; and no, they can't just do it with God. They must learn to be brutally honest with other men because when they can't feel God, they need someone to touch them. I think God pulls back a bit, ever so slightly, so that we can figure this out and learn our need for others.

Self-hatred has to die. The victim mentality must be killed, no whining allowed. The difference between being honest and complaining is the spirit behind it. If you're complaining, men will push away from you. If you're being real, they will be drawn to you and love you for it.

I like competition, so I always try to win the most vulnerable contest. We don't have an actual contest for that, but one is unofficially going on all the time. We're men, and yeah, everything is a competition. Create this culture in your group and you will be shocked at how deep you go each week and how quickly your men get better.

Actively Listen

There is a lot going on when you are listening to your men talk. Always remember that everything you do is being watched by the other men, and you are essentially training them in what works and what doesn't. It's on-the-job training and they are quick learners because their penises are very important to them, so you have their attention. They're scared and it's all new to them. The Holy Spirit is involved and drawing things out because he loves us too much to leave us the way we are. Every situation is different and he will give you insight because you have oversight. So listen to your men with one ear and to the Holy Spirit with the other.

Actively listen. Patton said, "You will be surprised at how much information you can get from someone if you act interested." Sit forward in your chair and look them in the eyes with an open body posture. Don't cross your arms or legs. Don't yawn, look away, exhale, rub your face, or let them catch you looking at your watch. This is their time and they are getting better just by having someone who cares listen to them. This is a first for many and it's exactly what they need.

As you listen to your men each week, collect information and store it. Gather prayer fodder for later. It's super easy to pray for people when you know what to go after. Listen for bad theology and lies that they believe.

> A little over two years ago, Jeff's son was killed in a small plane crash in Alaska. Just two weeks later he lost his wife to an illness. His grief was enormous. I can't even imagine. He had a great marriage, and the losses took him to a place sexually he didn't want to go.
>
> Broken up, he showed up at group, processed his grief, and found community. Jeff did the work, slowly came back to life, and got sexually pure again. He had an excellent group leader, Kevin, who later moved to China, and has since started a men's sexual purity group there.
>
> Jeff took over the group after Kevin left and his group has thrived. He is a father to the men in his group, they look up to him, and it's meeting a need in all of their hearts.
>
> Well over a year ago he met an amazing woman and they planned to be married. But since she is Canadian, they had a very long, drawn out, and complicated visa problem that held up a marriage license. So they waited. Rejecting advice to just get married and do the paperwork later, they have stayed pure. The visa finally came through, and they're very, very happily married and living on his ranch.

Saying What Is True

During the prayer time, do repeat-after-me statements that declare what is true, and you will see a lot of tears. For example if a man says, "I'm a loser" or "I'm worthless" when he's talking, sometime during the prayer time have him repeat the truth: "I am not a loser" or "I am highly valued." When you do this you straighten out what is broken in isolation in a public way and it is powerful. When the lie is spoken, it's broken. Saying it opens them up be loved and valued.

Find the Source of Pain

Let's talk about basic psychology. Even though I read a bunch of human psychology books in college, I learned this by working with horses: A man is what he is today because of his past. His past hurts and pains control his future if they are not faced, walked through, and healed. When we were kids we didn't have the tools to face what scared us, but now we are men and we do.

Facing our fears is still super scary, but it's the only option to get better. So listen for traumatic events in your men's pasts that they still carry today and that control what they do now. Trust me, those events are there, these guys didn't just come by their issues genetically; so look for the source of the pain and gently help them get it out and see it for what it is. Putting light on past pain they endured in isolation is healing. Words or prayers aptly spoken into the pain will bring the healing they need to be at peace and to change their future behavior.

Listen for broken relationship structures (for example, with mothers, fathers, peers—both male and female). Are the men giving away to others what they have been receiving? Do they have non-Christian friends? (We need these friendships too.) What hurts and what is missing in their relationships? Help them rebuild what is broken and to make things right with others as much as it's in their power to do so.

Ask for Help

Men need men to get better, period. They don't get a sponsor in a small group so they have to be the friend they would want to have. They need to get other men's phone numbers and call them before they screw up, not after. No one wants to be used as a confessional.

If a man isn't reaching out, ask him why; the majority of men have a tough time with this. One way to teach this is having guys say out loud, "I need help." I can't count how many men have cried over this when I have them do it. Asking for help and accepting help not only hasn't been taught, but we grew up on John Wayne and James Bond, and it's been subconsciously discouraged. When a guy calls me the first thing I say is, "Good job for making the call. Well done." Then I pray for him. Bam! He wins, you win, and it's all good because he is in the light, the isolation is broken, the connection is made, and the need of his heart is met.

To get out of the cycle of addiction men have to get the needs of their hearts met in a healthy way. This takes time because for the most part they themselves don't know what they need, so there is a long learning curve. Be patient, the rewards are huge, and these guys will love you for it.

Men at Work

Work is a huge part of getting better. It's telling how many men show up that are not working. This group will get them working again. I say things like, "I need you to get twenty job applications out this week, can you do that for me?" If they can't, I ask them not to come back. Men are made to protect and provide. If they are not doing that, I bring the heat until they do it or choose to leave.

Managing You

Listen for how the guys in your group manage themselves. How do they respond when they are emotionally taxed? An acronym to help you judge how they're doing is H.A.L.T.S. Hopeless, Angry,

Lonely, Tired, Stressed. Bored should also be in there, but I couldn't make it work in the acronym. Before a man does something stupid he will be feeling at least one of those emotions and many times most of them at once. What are your men doing to combat the things that set them off?

Some options are:
- take a nap
- call someone
- reduce workload or responsibilities
- find something that brings them life
- remind themselves what God has said about them

Teach them how to recognize the things that set them off and to adjust their behavior before they do something dumb that will cement how they are feeling and prolong the agony.

Never condemn failure, men will be hard enough on themselves, trust me, or they wouldn't be in the group. Failure is what you do just before you succeed. So ponder what happened, and go back and see when the slide down the slope happened. Help them to see it so they can make adjustments for next time, because there will most likely be a next time. Because you have time with these men, applaud even the slightest improvement. Encouragement is the fuel that propels purity.

Homework

Push the men in your group with homework each week until they figure out how to give themselves homework. Homework builds momentum by providing opportunities for small victories, which lay a foundation of success to build on. Momentum is crucial. Every man is tempted, but an idle man tempts the devil. Make sure the guys in your group are always working on something. The second thing out of each man's mouth each week, right after how he did sexually, should be how he did with his homework.

Here are some examples of good homework with the purpose of working toward purity:

1. Call three people this week and hang out with one of them outside the group.
2. Take a hike to a lake or waterfall and when you get there take a swim.
3. Go to sleep by 10 p.m.
4. Take your guitar out in the woods and worship.
5. Go fishing.
6. Cut out something that is dragging you down this week, for example, Internet, video games, alcohol, or Facebook.
7. Make some small step toward pursuing a dream this week.
8. Break off an unhealthy relationship or reestablish contact with an old friend.

Eat Together

If you want to be a great leader, feed your men. Men love food. The Alpha Course expanded all over the world and revived the Anglican church because their people ate together. Eating together is communion, it's intimate. You take food into your body and you share it with others. It feels good; it's family. So when you meet outside of the room, make sure there is food. Provide good food; don't ever bring a lame lamb to a sacrifice. The men will catch on to this good-food thing after a while and start asking what they can bring, and that is a good sign. Giving to others is one of the steps in getting free.

———

Some of you men are a little nervous to lead a group. That's okay; let that energy work for you. You will rise to the occasion and leading will get you better faster than sitting in a group. It will help you articulate what only rolled around in your head before. When Patton flew into North Africa to take over control of all the U.S. and Allied forces on the ground he said, "A man's spirit enlarges with responsibility." Yours will too.

These are the basics. Use them, refine them, and make them your own. Educate yourself. Some great books are *Falling Forward*, *Breaking Free*, *Wild at Heart*, *War as I Knew It*, and my favorite, *Get Naked*.[3] Let me remind you again to be focused on getting better yourself and always asking yourself, "Would I want to go to this group?" If the answer is yes, you're doing it right.

---

3. *Falling Forward* by Craig Lockwood, *Breaking Free* by Russell Willingham, *Wild at Heart* by John Eldredge, *War as I Knew It* by General George Patton.

3

GO BIG

NO MATTER HOW HARD YOU TRY TO KEEP THE GROUP QUIET, if you're doing it right, you won't be able to. Men that are getting sexually free and experiencing intimacy, friendship, love, and acceptance can't shut up because they are so happy. So be prepared to grow. Begin with the end in mind, and have a men's group that's so good it will make men love to come to church. We have that with our group, and this section tells how we did it. It's how we still do it. Yours will look different, because you're you and I am me. Learn from us; then go get it done. If you have the heart of the men, you have the heart of the church. If we can get that right, we'll change the world.

Growing Beyond One Small Group

When you're just starting, only meet for one hour, and only do small group. The day you get to eight men, split the group and give the new group to the best man you have. (The criteria we use to select group leaders are simple: married, but we'll go with a single guy in great shape on occasion, sober, committed, employed, and with the ability to lead.)

Once you split and have two small groups, everything starts to change. Now when you meet, start off with both groups together and do testimonies, then split up into your individual small groups after that. Good news corporately keeps the unity of the whole.

As men keep coming add them to the split groups until they reach seven men each. When these groups are full, again pick out your best man and start another group. The momentum of growth is fun to watch and be a part of. To grow well takes time and really comes down to developing great leaders. When you hit three groups, pull out the guitar. Keep worship short, maybe just a couple of simple songs (just enough for the men to get their hearts centered in the right place) and keep doing testimonies. As the group grows, slowly increase the time allotted for each segment and add the talk; games should be added to the schedule last.

The following is a functionality breakdown on how we run our church's men's group. Please adapt it and make it your own. This is what we've found works for us after many mistakes, failings, and adjustments.

We meet at 7 p.m. on Mondays—that's every Monday, holidays and all. And our general format goes something like this:

- Worship: 20 minutes with a short opener and closer.
- Game or Contest: 5 minutes, no more than 10 minutes.
- Testimonies: 5 minutes.
- Speaker: 30 minutes.
- Small Group: 1 hour.

WORSHIP

We worship just long enough for men to get their heads in the right place. Worship, if we're doing it right, brings us face to face with the living God. It peels away the junk from the day and gets us focused on Jesus. It creates expectancy in the room and in our hearts, reminding us that we're not in this alone. He is there to help us, save us, heal us.

We sing two, sometimes three simple songs that we all know in a key we can really belt out loud. I like songs that aren't too wordy, songs that have the word "holy" or "Jesus," songs that connect us with our deep need and desperation for him. Songs that remind us who he is, what he has done, and what he is about to do.

I want a worship leader who brings us into the presence of God. I don't particularly care as much how musically talented he is. I do very much care how anointed he is. Some of the most anointed worship leaders are some of the most honest and most broken men in the room.

> Quinton showed up at group a young man floating between high school and the next thing. He was looking at porn and living unpeacefully with consequences that come with it. His first night at group he was fully impacted and overwhelmed by the presence of God. He was put into Casey's small group. Although he knew God had miraculously set him free from the desire to look at porn or masturbate, he stayed in the group. He pushed in to being honest and vulnerable, built relationships, and did the homework Casey gave him to do each week.
>
> He started to lead worship for the group, and there is a huge anointing on him to lead men into the presence of God. He writes songs that rock me. His humility moves me. He has been sexually pure since the day he walked into the room three years ago. I like to be around Quinton because there is a holiness about him that leaks on to everyone he is with. He has since moved away to college in Southern California, where he started and leads a successful men's sexual purity group.

After we had been going for a few years, Jeremy, a friend of mine who is an excellent worship leader, moved to town and started leading unplugged in a real, honest, and pure way. The men in the room were really drawn to him. He put together teams and got a rotation going. He made a list of twenty-five songs and said, "Let's keep it simple and just sing these. We feel like men when we sing these songs, so let's stick to them." He fathered the other men in the room and really brought us to the point where we are today. It's some of the best worship I've ever been in.

Desperate worship is great worship. Worship is warfare and worshipers get well because worship is a relational act of intimacy with God; sexual sin is a counterfeit to that intimacy. Worship is the center of our relationship with God. When we worship well, we get well.

Gideon tore down the Asherah pole that belonged to his father and in the same place built an alter of worship.[1] He then led one of the greatest revivals in biblical history. Asherah poles were ancient pornography, carved wooden images of breasts and genitalia. He got rid of his dad's porn. He turned from his father's sin and replaced it with a place of worship.

Worship is crucial to our healing. It invites the presence of God that transforms lives. Great moves of God happen, both personally and corporately, when we purpose ourselves to worship. Above all else men, make worship a priority. When it's done well, we get well.

TESTIMONIES

Testimonies should be short, one minute, maybe two if they're great, three if we're all crying. They should be brief, honest, and in a nonreligious way say, "This is where I was. This is where I am now. This is how I got there. God is good."

The primary function of the testimony is to release hope: "Wow, that guy did it and he was really screwed up. If he did it, I can do it too." Testimonies say, if God did it once, he'll do it again. When the men tell fresh stories of getting better, week after week, the faith in the room rises. It's like fishing when everyone around you is catching fish. You start looking to see what bait they're using. How are they doing it? You start to fish confidently, and you start to catch fish too.

While your group is small, you can just call for testimonies from the front of the room and let whoever wants to talk have a minute. If you regularly have a lot of new guys, ask only for testimonies from guys that have been there for two months or more. Do not let big talkers take over. Make clear the boundaries on brevity and what you want to hear. If you know that someone has a great story this week, save that person for last and end there. If you call for

---

1. Judges 6–7.

random testimonies keep going until you hit a winner, then stop. If the first one is out of the park, great, just quit right there. You got what you were looking for.

Once our attendance grew to about 100 to 125 men, I noticed that I had a hard time just calling for testimonies and getting what I was looking for. It went on for weeks, it was like a desert. Then the reason why hit me, there were so many men in the room that guys didn't feel safe. Also, I had done some "don't toot your own horn—let someone else toot it for you" teaching recently. So, with my ear to the ground, I stopped calling for open testimonies and tapped men beforehand to ask them if they would tell a short testimony. I find the guys that are doing well just through normal conversation, or a group leader might say something to me about a guy in their group that is doing well, so I ask questions about him. I'm trying to get the guy with the best story up front every week, a man God just met, a man that will release hope in the room.

One very important thing is to ask a man to give a testimony only moments before he gets up in front of everyone. It doesn't give him time to think. What he ends up saying will be raw and straight from the heart, fresh and alive, giving freedom to all who hear it. When someone really brings it raw, I like to stand and clap for him and then get up there and brag on him profusely. On occasion I might highlight what he did right and use it not just as an injection of hope, but as a teaching moment. I am careful not to upstage the guys giving testimonies, but I show them the respect they deserve for a courageous act of honesty that sets other men free.

GAMES

This is big fun. Men love to compete. The day they stop competing, they're dead. A contest brings men to life, but there is deeper purpose in why we do what we do. Some games are physical and showcase talent or stamina like the one-handed push-up contest, the chair jump, or the hold your breath in a bucket of water contest. Other games get us over fear of rejection because we have to look stupid or show a side of ourselves or a talent we have that others would not have known about without the game. Some of our games work on working together like the bat relay, dodgeball, or the blindfolded chicken catching contest. Men get to enjoy the camaraderie of getting dirty together to achieve a goal. They have to communicate, strategize, and encourage one another. Games connect us to others. But more than anything they're fun. We laugh, slap high fives, and cheer wildly. We're men. Win or lose, it's beautiful because it's relational.

Another important function of the games we play is to recapture what was lost. Many men missed a lot of innocent fun growing up because they were preoccupied with sex, so they are emotionally underdeveloped. When we play a game later in life that we missed playing in junior high because we were chasing girls or porning out, it brings healing.

We always give away a prize. Napoleon said that if he would have had enough medals, he could have taken over the world. It's amazing what a man will do to win something. We have given away a lot of different things over the years but hands down, men like to win food. When food is the prize, the winner can eat it right now and share the spoils with his friends. I like to go with a box of cookies, some kind of chocolate, or the ever popular thirty-two ounce bottle of craft beer.

One limiting factor for a lot of games is time. Five to seven minutes is where you want to land. I really like playing dodgeball, but a couple of games will eat up twenty minutes. But we still need to play it, so it's a once a year thing. I do dodgeball on a night I'm speaking and shorten my talk. Some things are important to do even if they are long, but generally I'm working real hard to keep it short. You can have a good laugh and a lot of fun in five minutes.

Play music that matches the contest with each game. I listen to mostly country, so that is usually what I play. It gets guys pumped up and sets the mood, making the experience that much better.

PART THREE GO BIG

Joe grew up in the desert out in the middle of nowhere. He was socially awkward when he came to group and had never dated a girl. He told me later that I offended him on his first night to group, but he refused to let that stop him. He kept coming. He showed up with the standard single guy penis control problems. But he went after it, all in.

He is one of the hardest working guys I know. He'll work himself into a sweat over the most menial tasks. He will play nearly every game we do if you let him. He asks questions and is looking for answers. He didn't know it at the time but he mostly came looking for friends. He found them. The men in his small group launched him forward in getting better. His consistent interactions with them help burn off his relational anxiety.

Last year was a big year for him. He got his penis under control and led a group. When he fixed my ATV and did such a surprisingly good job in such a short time, I asked him if he had his own tools. He said he had some tools. I told him he might try and put an ad up on Craigslist advertising as a mobile mechanic and see what happens. His phone started ringing off the hook and shortly after, he quit his busboy job. He has since made plenty of mistakes, but he's not just making it, his business is growing. He was given a really nice used truck, bought a mobile tools trailer, is buying more tools, and he is even splitting the rent on a shop in town with three other guys.

This spring, while working together out in the shop, I realized he had never traveled anywhere...ever. So I shot out a quick idea for a working/traveling-around-the-U.S. motorcycle trip. He jumped on it and left a few months later driving by the house to say good-bye. The last call I got from him, he was in Oregon having the time of his life.

The point is, men, when you get your penis under control by being honest and building relationships, things start to come together. You come alive and get the desires of your heart.

Sexual purity groups have this dark-church-basement reputation. Forget that, we're having fun out in the sunshine. Games bring the cool to the misconceptions.

Here are some of the games we play, how we play them, and why. We've done a bunch more but these are our best, tried and true, and very fun. They are listed in groups: physical, vulnerable, developmental, and relational. And they're all just plain fun. Rotate the category of game from week to week to let different guys with different talent levels have a chance to win.

Physical Prowess and Contests of Strength

Guys need to burn off steam. How much better is it if they get to win something they can eat in front of (or share with) men they love.

> **Push-up or Sit-up Contest.** A variation is the one-handed push-up contest. Have everyone start together. Each man has a counter who puts his fist on the ground to make sure the player goes down low enough to touch the counter's fist with his chest. On the sit-up competition, we have the players do sit-ups on an angle, using the stairs to the stage, so they're really hard to do. The counter holds the player's feet. For the one-handed push-ups, I let the players switch hands one time. I am regularly amazed at how many one-handed push-ups these guys can do. It's a respect thing in the room for sure. For these games I like to give out smaller second and third place prizes as well.
>
> **Breath Holding Contest.** Get some five gallon buckets, fill them almost full with water and line them up. The men competing should get on their knees and stick their faces up to just before their ears in the water (so they can hear). Count off in fifteen second intervals and also let them know how many men are left so each player knows where he stands. It gets pretty cool near the end as everyone is yelling out encouragement.

PART THREE **GO BIG**

Chair Jump. Line up three chairs and get as many volunteers as you can. Give the guys a big running start and keep adding one chair to the line after everyone clears it. You'll have some great wipeouts and loud cheering.

Hot Dog, Banana, or Watermelon Eating Contest. These are a big hit with the single guys in the room. Plus they get free food.

Water Bottle Grab. Get some empty water bottles and pile them up on one side of the room. Line up the men who want to play on the other side and have one less water bottle than there are men playing each time. When you say go, the guys playing run and grab a bottle. It turns into a big dog pile and is super funny. Whoever doesn't come up with a bottle is out. Keep removing one bottle and eliminate one guy each time you go. Mix it up a little bit by changing the way they can go get the bottle, like hop on one leg, crawl, roll, or run backward.

Vulnerability Games

These games push all kinds of insecurity buttons because they can make us look dumb in front of people. Just getting up there in front of everyone is a risk that leads to getting better. These games show something about ourselves that risks rejection because we have to show other men a part of who we are that few have ever seen.

Hairy Chest Contest. A variation is the Hairy Back Contest. Another good one is the Who Has the Least Amount of Hair Contest. Get a line of guys up front and have them take off their shirts one at a time to the applause of the room. The winner will be obvious and crowd response is the best part of the game.

Dance Contest. This is one of my all-time favorites and we have several different ways we do it. One way is to get some guys up front and play a fifteen-second montage of popular dance songs from each decade. Another way that will get some great laughs is to have each player pick a song he wants to dance to, then tell everyone the song and put earphones on the dancer so he can hear the music but everyone else can't. Hilarious. Another good one is to just have them say the song they are going to dance to but not play any music, so it's just one guy at a time, cold on the stage singing the music in his head and dancing. Super funny. Air guitar is another form of dance contest that's a huge hit as well. Just get a bunch of guys up in front and play something with a great guitar solo and let them go at it. It's a great laugh.

Screaming Contest. Go down to the thrift shop and buy a bunch of ten-cent t-shirts so guys can rip them off as they scream as loud as they can. The best Tarzan yell is a good one too. You might show a video of Tarzan yelling in the jungle to get them inspired. Extra points for beating your chest.

Body Building Contest. Once you get the guys up front, have them take off their shirts and rub on some baby oil. Then play some funky 70s music while they flex their muscles. This is a riot. The best built guys never win this game. It's the performance that gets the applause. Great laughs too.

Singing Contest. Give each man fifteen to twenty seconds to sing a song of his pick, no music. You'll be surprised and deeply moved at how good men sing. They don't even have to sing well, it's just that they did it. There won't be much, if any, laughter but there will be a lot of applause. It's great. For great laughs do a singing contest called iPod Idol. Each player picks a song from the list, then puts the earphones on to sing it. He thinks he's singing great, but it's very often way off tune. Plus he's up there dancing to the music while he sings it. Hilariously huge laughs.

Developmental Games

These are what you missed out on as a kid and we're recapturing that which was lost. These games are mostly pretty dumb, but they're awfully fun.

Blindfolded Shoe Hunt. Have about ten guys or so take off their shoes. Put the shoes in a pile. Then move the players about twenty yards away. Have them close their eyes and race to find their own shoes. When they put their shoes back on, they then have to go jump into an assigned person's arms (this person is hiding in the room somewhere) to win. The big laughs happen when there is a pile of guys wrestling over a pile of shoes.

PART THREE GO BIG

The Big Swinging Cucumber. You need empty soda cans, string, and cucumbers. Tie the string around each player's waist and tie the cucumber to the other end of the string so it is hanging straight down between his legs. The object is to use the swinging cucumber to knock the empty soda can along the ground across the finish line that is about thirty yards away. Play some music while they do it. Big fun.

Burping Contests. These are quick and good for a laugh. Have some soda to drink to help with the burping.

Eating Live Fish Bait. This is always a huge hit. We've done a bunch of different styles of play with this game—the best one we call, Mother Hen. Guys come up and flap their arms like wings and say, "cheep, cheep," like they are baby birds and want food to eat. Then we grab something that is a total surprise to them out of the bag and feed it to them. Start slow and build up. Go with a raw egg first, then a night crawler, a grub, a live minnow, and finish with a crayfish. The crowd will go wild with amusement. Have a trash can nearby in case anyone needs to puke.

Drink a Soda Through a Sock. You can do it with clean socks, their own socks, or if you're feeling more adventurous, have them put their own sock over the can and at the last moment have them switch cans so they have to drink through someone else's sock. There will be a collective moan from the crowd. Very fun.

Eat a Cookie Off Your Forehead. This is a good quick game that gets a good laugh. Have whoever wants to play sit in a line of chairs with their heads tilted back. Place a large cookie on each of their foreheads. They have to eat the cookie without it falling to the ground and without using their hands. Hysterical.

Donut on a String. Get a board or a broom handle and tie twelve strings to it. Then get a dozen donuts and tie them on the hanging end of each string. The strings should be close enough that the donuts barely touch. Have two men hold up the broom handle. This is a donut eating contest and you can't use your hands or drop the donut. Play some music while the players eat and have a good laugh while they smash donuts all over each other's faces. You might bring some wipes or paper towels too.

Naked Man Musical Chairs. It's musical chairs with a twist. Have those playing put their shirts and pants on a chair so they're just in their boxers. The players walk around the circle of chairs and when the music stops they have to put on whatever clothes are on the chair as fast as they can and sit down. Last guy down is out. Keep going till you have a winner. The comedy here is the off-size of the clothes guys have to put on.

Inch Worm. Have the guys who want to play strip down to their boxers and wrap them each in cellophane as tight as you can with their feet together and arms by their sides. Then lay them in a line and put a banana on a plate for each player about twenty yards away. The players have to inch their way, like a worm, over to the banana and eat it. First one done wins. You will laugh hard.

Relational or Team Games

These are great for connecting guys. These games break isolation and get us talking. They teach us to work together and get us close to people. It's more fun to win together.

Tug-O-War. Have all the men take off their shirts. Then split the room in half by hairy chests verses non-hairy chests. We do this every year and I have been on the no hair side. No hair is up two to one.

Dodgeball. You know what to do. For the sake of time don't let anyone come back in the game. Once you're out of the game, you're out. Ways to split the room are by odd or even birthdays, or by young guys vs. the old guys.

Bat Relay. Get in teams relay style. One guy from each team runs about forty yards or so, picks up a baseball bat, and spins around ten times with his head on the bat and the bat touching the ground. Have a counter for each team count each spin out loud. The fun starts when the players try to run back to their lines. Because they're so dizzy there are a lot of great wipeouts. Keep going until everyone in the line has had a turn.

Football Toss. I like to do this one around Super Bowl time. Each guy playing gets a partner. One partner stands on the stage or up high on something; he should put his ankles together and stand bow-legged. The other partner, from about twenty yards out, tries to throw the football between his legs. He gets extra points if the ball passes through close to his partner's tenders. Yes, someone usually gets hit there…

Goat Milk Relay. I have some milk goats, so I bring a couple of them for this game. Have teams line up in relay lines. Players have to run down to the goats and lie on their backs while a teammate squirts milk straight from the goat into their mouths. When the player's mouth is full he has to run back and spit the milk into a cup. The team who fills its cup first wins. I wish I would have taken a picture of all the shocked faces the first time I did this. The guys got through the shock and it has been one of our best games ever.

Blindfolded Chicken Catching Contest. This is my all-time favorite game. All you need is a chicken; a rooster is preferable. Find a small fenced area. We use one that is about forty-five by forty feet that works perfectly. Let the chicken go in the fenced area. Have each man playing get a partner. One guy is blindfolded and the other is following right behind him (without touching him) telling him where to go and how to catch the chicken. I'm not sure how I came up with this game, but the first time we did it I laughed until my stomach hurt. The chicken naturally moves away from people; like a good running back he'll even shoot the gaps and go into the open area. All the guys playing look really slow as they grab for a chicken that is not there. Not to fear though, participants usually figure it out in a few minutes, holding the bird up to loud cheers.

Cheetos Feet Feed. Get a bag of big Cheetos and some paper plates. Have the men playing grab a partner. Count out ten Cheetos for each team and put them on a plate. One guy lies down and the other, with his bare feet, feeds him five Cheetos. When he's done with the five, they switch places. First team done wins. It is awkwardly funny to watch guys with toe lint try to get a Cheeto in the other guy's mouth. You will laugh.

This list isn't exhaustive, but you get the idea. Use what works for you and make up your own. The main point is that men like to play and get dirty. They look forward to the game each week. It's an ice-breaker that gets us into real time. Keep the games short and shocking. Praise the winner and encourage the guys who had the courage to get up front and make fools of themselves. We heal better together and men just need something to do. A lot of the time, guys are just stuck, and winning can give them a good lift. I have noticed over the years that the men who get up front and play the most games are often the men who get better faster.

When doing a game, I explain what we're going to do and what the rules are. Then I show off the prize and explain the criteria for winning. In the physical or team games, the winner is usually clear. But in the vulnerable or developmental games, it's subjective, so the winner is determined by applause. If there were twenty guys in the screaming contest, I would bring up the top three to five guys at the end and have a scream off and then ask all the guys in the audience to cheer for their favorite.

To start a game I call for volunteers. If I don't get enough, I keep selling it until I do. If we're playing a game that's a little scary and we're still short then I will hit them with, "There's method in my madness. There is a reason we're playing this game. It's for you to get better on the inside, and now is your chance." I tell them David, a man after God's own heart, danced in his jockstrap in front of the whole city and teenage girls. He did it, you can do it too. Often the same guys will want to come up each week, which is fine, but I might discourage them on occasion just to have some new blood up there. Every now and then I'll say only the guys who have never played a game can play this one, just to break new guys out of their shells.

TALK

Talks should be short. If you are just getting started, don't have a talk at all, just do the small group. When you split to two groups, go with five-minute talks and keep moving up the time as you grow. No matter how big you get, talks should never be more than thirty minutes. Men, for the most part, will pass on long speakers. They want it said and done. Out of the fifty-two weeks of the year we have about seven outside speakers come in (half of those speakers are women) and we give them forty-five minutes.

The job of the speaker is to bring us face to face with God. Speakers tell us the truth and are dangerously honest. They show humility and speak with confidence. They are teachers and storytellers. They use metaphor and their own experience. Their lives may be a mess, but they are getting better. They make us laugh. They often cry when they speak. They show us what is possible with God.

Our pulpit is a special place. You can't fake it up there. If you try, the men in the room can smell it a mile away. We have had several outside speakers who regularly speak to thousands of people come in and choke because the atmosphere of honesty is daunting. The men in the room are at a turning place in life. Many are hurting and being vulnerable for the first time, facing their hurt to heal. They are very raw. They need someone to connect with them in that place and be raw too.

I was a communication major in college and focused on public speaking. I was good at it. When I came to Christ my junior year, I was undone. Within months I completely lost all ability from the podium. I became so insecure that it was difficult to speak to more than a few people. I've got a long and painful story here, but the short of it is, it took me twenty years to dig myself out of that hole and be comfortable to speak publicly again. I didn't check out, I kept taking opportunities to speak when offered, but there were more losses than wins for a long time. God broke me down, and it

Brian's wife Raina came home from a great night out with some of her girlfriends to find out that Brian had been looking at porn. The guilt was all over his face. Over the years in their marriage, he had done the only thing he knew to do and that had been white-knuckling it (meaning, just trying really hard not to do it), but porn kept pulling him down and hurting their relationship. Raina was angry. She asked him what he was going to do about it because she didn't want it to ever happen again. That's when Brian showed up to group.

Brian had friends, locationships mostly, but he needed guys he could go deeper with. He found that in the group, got honest, and got free. He figured out what was going on inside and dealt with his heart, and not just his outward performance. This was a cool jump to see him make as he is a very self-disciplined person; the porn problem was the pressure point that made him dig deep enough to get better from the inside out.

Today Brain has one of the best marriages I know. His wife also started and runs a group for the wives of the men in the group. They pray for their husbands, support each other, and she helps women work through the tough stuff. It's pretty cool. Last year we had her in to speak and she was one of our best speakers. She fully killed it.

Brian is our longest standing small group leader. He's great at it too as he has been doing it for over five years now. His dreams are coming alive as well. He is a zero body fat type of guy and he just started his own fitness business that's very unique and super cool. It is diet-related, with caveman workouts out in nature: climbing cliffs, lifting logs, running through water, throwing rocks. It's great.

Now that porn isn't stealing his energy and focus, he can put his energy back into his own life and responsibilities as a father, husband, and provider. He is finally having traction and success. He has found what is bringing him life. He is doing it, and it's working.

took two decades to rebuild me in this area. I wouldn't want to do it again, but I'm glad it went the way it did. It's much less about the speaking than actually having something to say. Jonah had heat on what he had to say after being in the belly of the whale.[2] I wonder if Nineveh would have repented if he would have skipped the three-day belly of the whale ride. There has never been a good message that someone didn't suffer for. It's the price of great preaching.

Through the rebuilding process I learned a lot. Today one of my favorite, most satisfying things to do is to work with our speakers to make them better. I'm not running a charity. I put the best man in the room up to speak each week, but I work with him, a little before, and a little after. If I'm trying a new guy who has something to say, it's my job to help him get it out. I spend a lot more time with the new guys than with the more seasoned speakers.

Before you put a new guy up, let him open and close worship a few times. Let him lead the testimony time or give his own. Give him some exposure in the front so he feels the room and starts to build a connection.

I often pull up a guy I believe in and split a talk with him for his first time. If he screws it up, I can clean it up and it's all good. The best speaker we have ever had in the group fully messed up his first talk. He was barely coherent. I put him up the next time in the summer on a holiday (I wasn't there because I take summers off) and I heard from everyone that he completely killed it. He was off and running after that, failure is part of getting good at something.

When picking who will speak, you're the head chef and you want to serve a balanced meal. Create the best meal possible, and not just for taste or for the presentation. You want organic, nutrient-dense ingredients, high in protein, and raw. Look for guys who have the heat on them, those whom God is at work in their lives, guys that are yielding to him and getting results.

It's very important to me that the man on the pulpit has a good marriage that is getting better. I want to know that he and his wife

---

2. Jonah 1–3.

are aggressively working on their stuff, and that he is making decisions primarily with his family in mind. If you can see new life, hope, and excitement in the eyes of a man's wife, you know he's doing well. If a man is single, I look to see that he's determined to deal with his stuff—it's preparation for the family that is to come. To find the guys with the heat on them, I listen to what others are saying. I look for men who are leading by example and who are being followed by others, and for men who may fail, but are quick to humbly repent and get back at it. These are the men I want to hear speak.

Here is my regular talk with a new speaker: Find out what you want to say. Then take the plane off, fly straight, then land the plane. It takes preparation and energy to take off, flying straight isn't too tough, but the most important thing you will do is land the plane. You might not have a perfect handle on everything that comes out of your mouth and in what order, but know how you will begin and more importantly how you will end.

To me, a great speaker (for what we're doing) is based on how often he can bring a good word. You can find and work with great guys, but how often can they be great is the question. You have to find the line of frequency that is the right timeline for each man. The best speakers in the room are right at, or just under the two month mark. Several are at the three month mark, others are twice a year, and a handful only speak once in the summer. If you put a guy up too early, and if he hasn't fully processed what he needs to, what he says will come out choppy. If you wait too long, you miss the sweet spot and he is already on to the next thing and his message loses its heat because he is pulling it up from the past.

I don't control or direct the speakers. I try to help them pull out what is already there if they need it. When I give the pulpit away, it's the speaker's time and I trust him with it. I give a lot of encouragement, as speaking is a courageous act. If someone bombs (which doesn't happen very often) they know it, nothing needs to be said. I just love them. It's easy for me since I have bombed more than anyone I know. Love and acceptance brings out the best in us all.

SMALL GROUP

The details of the small group are covered in the previous section, but there are a few more things that need to be addressed here regarding doing small group within the context of a larger men's group.

Be careful not to steal time from small group with longer segments of worship, testimonies, games, or talks. This is very important. We give small groups an hour and many take a little more time by leaving a little later. Some groups will meet before and eat together, other groups might go have a beer, or a barbecue after the speaker is done. This is all great and encouraged; however doing stuff together is not a replacement for doing small group. Respect the group time, that's where your men get better.

We don't try and figure out who goes in what group—it's just a God lottery. The first six guys to show up ready to start in a group are usually put into a group together. I like really diverse groups best, but the Holy Spirit brings who he brings when he brings them, so we roll with that.

If someone has a complaint about a group down the road, I look at it, but most often I bring it back to the fact that God's leading is a factor in how groups are formed, and that man came at the time he did in response to that leading to be with these specific men for their healing. Like them or not, those are the cards you were dealt, so play them. Many times it's the tough guys in the group that can bring the most healing. They push buttons in the other guys in the group that bring stuff up and make guys have to face it. It's uncomfortable and messy, but healing and beautiful.

No matter how big your group grows in numbers or how your responsibilities increase, no one in the room should ever be above leading a small group or being in a small group. I lead a small group of new guys every year, just like the man next to me. Every time I sit down with a new group of guys, I'm never

Taylor showed up to group right out of high school, drowning in pornography. He ended up in a great group of older guys who were all struggling deeply with their own stuff. Seeing what decades of porn had done to the other men's lives, Taylor was impacted heavily and resolved to do whatever it took to get better. As he sobered up, he entered into a long season of pain. He would call guys all the time to get prayer, but when it was too late at night and no one would answer the phone, he would drive to the prayer house at church that is open 24/7 and cry his eyes out.

Taylor and his father, who is a pastor, had a very disconnected relationship. As Taylor got better, he wanted more in his relationship with his dad and told him everything. He poured out his heart starting with his sexual struggles. When he was done, his father was blown away, and in turn told him his own sexual struggles; the two have been very close ever since.

His dad was so moved by the event that he called and emailed me several times to thank me. He even loaded up some men from his church and made the long pilgrimage here, just to see what we were doing that had helped his son so much. Shortly after, those same men started a very successful sexual purity group in their church.

Taylor was in a long-term relationship with the love of his life. Together, they fully committed to purity and their relationship thrived. A year later they were married on the beach in a beautiful ceremony. I love to see them together as there is such a pure innocence about them and their friendship is strong.

I usually recommend (because of Deuteronomy 24:5) that newly married guys take a year off from group. Taylor would have none of it and didn't want to stop coming. He argued that what he did in group was a lifestyle that wouldn't change if he came to group or not. I gave in, and gave him a group to lead, which turned out to be excellent for everyone involved.

He has since moved back to his hometown. His wife is going to college, he is working, doing life, and helping to lead the sexual purity group in his church. They just bought a puppy, which is often what you do right before you have kids.

too excited about it, but I know I need to do it. Two months later, I'm in love with those men. Their lives improving, along with my own, is my reward.

We could do worship, teaching, games, and testimonies all night long every day of the week, but men would not get better without being in a group. It's relational practice. It's preparing you to be a better father and a better man so that you can live out to fullest what God has for you. Twenty years from now people will study us and how we did what we did. If they do their homework right, they will realize it was done through relationship.

Small Group Leaders

What we are doing only works with great group leaders. The only things I promise our leaders are free food, that they will get better, and that by leading a group they will get better faster. It's a volunteer army and I continually beat the drum for them to come to group for themselves, not to be a ministry leader, or to climb the religious ladder. The better they get, the more influence they will have. They change the world by changing themselves.

The best way to get good at leading is by watching and experiencing the leadership of someone who is good at it doing it, and then doing it yourself. But here is a hot tip. Hang around after group and catch the men who are good at leading and ask them for help. Run situations by them and ask what they would do. There are great leaders in the room, make use of them.

Once a month or so we have a small group leader feed (notice I didn't use the word meeting). We get together an hour before group and eat together. For maybe five or ten minutes of that time I will address what we're doing right and thank them for leading a group because it doesn't work without them. I'll also touch on things we can work on by saying something like, "Some of you guys are getting out of group too late. Keep it to five minutes each per man," and then spend a little time on why that's important. We'll also listen to other group leaders talk about successes and failures and what they learned. The leader feed is a cool monthly event that the men like coming to. It's like a trip behind the lines for a hot meal before they head back to the front.

LARGE GROUP DYNAMICS

Plain and simple men, this is combat and passive men don't get free. Tearing down strongholds is an act of violence.[3] Learn from those who have gone before us. Find the best and hang out with them. Get around them and let yourself be influenced. Read everything relevant you can get your hands on. Readers are leaders. Take comfort in the great and sometimes lesser known military leaders of the past. You will be surprised at how similar the experience of combat is to running a group and will take courage from their words. Some of my favorites are Patton, Ariel Sharon, Thomas Cochrane, Daniel Morgan, Lawrence of Arabia, Napoleon, Horatio Nelson, and David.

One thing to add here is that it is very important to have a peer in the room when you're leading the large group, someone who knows you and complements what you're doing. This person needs to have enough relational change with you to be able to point out problems or weak spots. Hold the vision, but listen to everything he says, because he has insight that you don't.

When the group really starts to grow and the intimacy is deep, the worship is moving, the honesty is uncomfortably beautiful and freeing, this is when you really start having church. Your group can/will start to feel more like the church than the church. At this point, make sure you don't reject the church in any way. It's very important that we never become an Absalom or raise a hand against the Lord's anointed.[4] You might be in a bad place and catch

---

3. 2 Corinthians 10:4.
4. 2 Samuel 16–18, 1 Samuel 24.

PART THREE GO BIG

> At over three years of sobriety, Adam holds the record for longest stretch for a single guy ever in the room. Two things are impressive about his streak. One is that he was really screwed up when he showed up. The other is that he met, and was engaged to great girl. They postponed their wedding twice, then called it off. Through that heart wrenching break up, he stayed pure and showed great integrity toward his fiancé.
>
> Last year he moved away, started his own business, and started a men's sexual purity group in his church. He called me today for advice as his church had just asked him to be on staff. He is an evangelist for holiness. He is ready to talk about it with anyone, anytime. He's not just sober, he's free. He hangs out with incredibly beautiful women and treats them like sisters. He can go dancing, have a few beers, stay connected with his friends, and be fine on the inside. Adam is fun to be around; he loves the Lord, and is sincere in his friendships. He gets that relationships are key in healing, hope, and happiness.

the king taking a crap, cut off a piece of his robe, and wave it around, but you'll get convicted for it. After twenty plus years of Jesus freaking, I have recognized that it doesn't go well for men who reject the church. So when the chips are down, no matter how bad it hurts, never reject the church. Repeat after me, never reject the church.

There will sometimes be church politics, misunderstandings, and pastoral concerns. It's just life in the trenches. Adjust your methods if needed, and work on your word choices, but don't water things down. If there is a problem, make sure that you're not it. Leading and running a group is difficult, but never boring. It's a challenge that is worth the effort. Be patient. Time and the fruit of changed lives make everything come out in the wash.

Leadership Structure

Leadership in the room should be natural. The leaders are who the leaders are—they don't need titles. Leadership teams get in the way of relationship. We're the Knights of the Round Table, everyone has equal input. The weight of a leader's influence is equal to the fruit of his life and his commitment to the overall betterment of the men in the room.

I liken our leadership in the room to what David did outside the walls of Jerusalem, before the Israelites captured it and made it their home. He looked around and said, "Who wants to be the leader? Whoever goes in there and kills the most Jebusites is the leader." A Jebusite represents sexual sin as it holds the very place in which we were meant to worship. Joab was the first in and received the command. Then David rebuilt the city, which became the central place of worship for all Israel.[5] Our leaders are those who do the same. They take ground, create a place to worship, and rebuild.

Men who need help should reach out on their own initiative and pull on other men whom they respect. They do this by asking questions while serving their leader (helping him wash his car, change out a battery, etc.), listening to his answers, then doing what he says. If you're going to ask your leader for advice and you get some, make a smart move and do what he says, even if you don't understand it, he does. A Jebusite killer has been there before, he knows what to do. Listen and act. The student should pursue the mentor not the other way around.

For what we do, and the way we do it, I like a strong central leader. This is the guy who runs the group and has no problem giving it up if someone, over time, is more qualified than he is. He holds on lightly, yet is deeply committed to the men. He listens to everyone, and can quickly implement changes when needed without a committee. He is ever learning through the lives of others and from his relationship with God. He is there to heal himself; he hasn't arrived. He is humble and confident in the call on his life. He

---

5. 1 Chronicles 11:4–9.

makes the final and prayerfully weighed decisions, and lives with the fallout. He loves the men, and they love him back. He honors the church and lives gracefully, on occasion, with misunderstanding. He protects the confidentiality of the men in the room. He gives strength to those who fail. He can acknowledge it when he himself fails. He loves Jesus, his family, and his church, and is a good provider. He is on a mission to get better and take as many men with him as possible.

Naaman, a great man and commander of an army, had leprosy and came to Elisha to be healed.[6] He showed up with his entourage, and Elisha told him to go take a dip in the sewer and he would be healed. He got mad, but was smart enough to listen to the friend who talked him into taking the swim. It was an act of humility that got him healed. Likewise men, we have to swallow our pride and get down in the sewer to get clean.

Money

The reward in leading a group is eternal treasure. It's satisfying to play a role in changing the direction of a man's life. I regularly get emails, texts, and calls from men, (locally, from around the country, and now internationally) thanking me for building a place where they could get better. The overwhelming theme is: "Thank you, you saved my life."

Treasure in heaven is a great reward but the light bill needs to be paid too. Here's our story, yours will be different because of the church you're in and the way you do things.

We ran the group for almost three years and got up to around seventy-five men with nothing more than an occasional donation. I was very clear when we started, and still am today, that we do this group in the church. That means we run our money through the church, we meet in the church, and have no intention of becoming a parachurch organization.

Today, we charge a one time fee of 150 dollars, and ask for a

---

6. 2 Kings 5.

six-month commitment. I wrestled with charging a fee for a long time and expected provision from other places, but it was pretty lean. I talked to my pastoral oversight at the time, and they both said I should start charging. One suggested a small amount of five dollars a week. I went with a variation of that with the one time fee, and it's worked really well for us. I was really uncomfortable charging for about six months, and then the light went on and we haven't looked back.

When men have to pay up to fix a problem they can't manage on their own, it's a humbling experience. That humility and desperation gets them where they need to be to start the process of getting better. When a guy turns in the paperwork and his check, he has skin in the game. He's not just checking it out anymore, he's going for it. The fee really helps with the commitment level, and it helps us pay the bills, so it's good both ways. I would recommend that you run your group at no cost until you build some good momentum. At least a year, two may be better. We started charging around about two and three-quarters years into it. In retrospect, right at two years in would have been best.

We spend our money on food for the small group leader feeds that we have once a month just before group. The games often need materials, and we always give away a prize. Also, all outside speakers get paid. Some have refused to take money, which is very cool, so we'll slip them a gift card to their favorite restaurant or something that fits them, just to honor them for coming in. We also pay our regular speakers in the group and it feels really good to do that, as great speaking is hard work, and they pay a price. So we meet that with a Ben Franklin or two.

Getting paid to run the group never crossed my mind in the early years. I certainly didn't start it with that in mind. Into the fourth year, because of our growth, there started being a surplus. So I was able to receive a small amount each month, as I have kids to feed too. I am self-employed, and have been the vast majority of my life, so it was weird at first, but then later it became nice to receive. Later that year my pastoral oversight arranged that our church would start to help monthly as well and added some acorns to the tree, so that was really nice. Shortly after that, donations started to come in. I am very grateful for all of it.

So here we are, running a successful and mostly self-sustaining group that feels great to go to each week. It takes time to get there, but we're changing lives, creating and sustaining both personal and corporate revival, and blessing the families within our church at the same time. It's a good deal.

An excellent financially freeing suggestion is to take an offering a few times a year. It's good for men to give. We find a worthy cause that is relationally connected, tell the story, and pass the hat. I am regularly surprised at the generosity. It's fun to give it away. It's one of my favorite things to do. Giving is an act that helps break the selfish, addictive mind-set.

Moving On, or Not

The cool part about the group—why I keep coming and why men who get what is going on don't leave—is that we keep getting better together. What we do in the room becomes a lifestyle; it's not just a check-this-off-the-list fulfillment of a program. The deeper we dig, the better relationships we have and the more sexually free we become. There are levels to our sexual freedom. It starts with getting sober and keeps going deeper and deeper. Through it we get to know and love ourselves more and more over time. Each deeper place you go makes you feel lighter, happier, and stronger. That's why I keep doing it, and other men do the same.

I don't ever pressure anyone to stay. Leave freely whenever you want to. This is a voluntary army. A bunch of guys move every year when school is over, so we expect that. On average we lose one leader a year who is just done coming, and I'm good with that. Most are so hooked by the process and intimacy in the room and can't find a replacement for it elsewhere, so they stay. Plus as you're getting better, so are the men you are leading in your small group. It's really rewarding to see their lives change, their marriages get better, prosperity at work in their lives, and the healing and reestablishing of their relationships. The pay is good and eternal.

There is a lot of talk about abortion, STDs, child pornography, and sex slavery, and a lot of great people doing some pretty positive things to combat these problems, as well they should. But with that said, the things on that list are all symptoms of the problem. When the demand is gone, the supply will be gone as well. By continuing to push in and pursue purity we change ourselves and the atmosphere around us. By changing us, we change the world.

MAN-I-FEST

Man-i-Fest is a weekend when our group as a whole goes up to a local campground to have some fun. We bring in an outside speaker, eat some great food, and enjoy some mountain air. Guys look forward to it all year. Last year the big hit was the Highland Games. We painted our faces blue, threw spears, flipped logs, heaved boulders, and carried weights for long distances. We had a giant slip and slide, a manually operated bull to ride, and a huge relay race that featured some of the best games of the year at once.

It's good to get out of town and be together. It's pretty cool after eating a pound-of-meat-per-person barbecue to have a bunch of men worshiping together around a big bonfire with an ice-cold river running fifty feet away in the background. It's just good for the heart, it re-centers you, and you come down from the mountain knowing the guys in your small group in a whole new way.

We have alumni leaving and starting groups all over the country, a handful internationally. They are all invited back to Man-i-Fest each year, and it's like a big family reunion. It's very encouraging to hear the testimonies, and to see God's hand on men as they live holy and with their lives influence others toward purity.

Last year we started letting non-alumni attend for the first time, the criteria being that they had to have a group going in their home church. If this is you, and you would like to come, just watch for the dates and info on our website (www.puritypursuit.com), and email us if you're interested. We are excited about the future as we can feel the momentum build. Where we're headed as men together feels good.

YOU TOO

A few years back a few friends and I went to a U2 concert in Oakland. Our seats were on the lower part of the upper level and once we found them, two guys sat down, and I went with another friend to grab some drinks. On the way back, coming out of the tunnel to get into the arena, I was moved by the sea of people and the energy in the air, as it was in between the warm-up band and U2 coming out on stage. In the moment, I saw my two friends at our seats and raised my arms and shouted, "HEY!!!" I was surprised to see about ten other people in our section stand up with their arms in the air and yell, " HEY!" right back at me.

Without thinking I yelled, "Let's start a wave!" I counted off and got about 100 people going. The next time, we were up to about 1,000. Now starting to lose my courage, I thought to myself, "I'll give it one more try." This time we got the whole upper level going (probably more than 10,000 people), but the wave didn't pass the break in the stadium to make it fully around. I was thinking, "Well that's it. Nice try," when somebody, way up in the back, yelled, "DON'T GIVE UP, YOU CAN DO IT!" With my courage renewed, I went for it one more time with a new passion. I even ran with the wave for a long time after starting it. The wave made it past the stadium break this time and all the way around. It increased in intensity and then started on the next level down, then the next level down started too. We were doing it together, but each level was at a different speed, going round and round, louder and louder. It was beautiful, and I had a moment.

People were coming from all over our section to pat me on the back and say, "Good job. Way to go! We knew you could do it." The wave went on longer than any I have ever seen, it just kept going and going, and it didn't stop until Bono stepped onto the stage. People were having fun, and I was a proud father.

The dream, gentlemen, is a men's purity group in every church on the globe. A place where men find a home and a family inside a local church body. Great victories are won when one man like Shammah gets tired of running and defends a field of beans.[7] He didn't have much but he defended what he had, turning the tide of the battle and bringing about a great victory.

It's time for a group in your church and you're the man for the job. Your church and the men in it need one man to defend a field of beans and turn the tide. They need one man to stand up and yell, "HEY!!!" And another, at just the right time, to say, "DON'T GIVE UP, YOU CAN DO IT."

---

7. 2 Samuel 23:11.

FIVE SMOOTH STONES

I WROTE GET NAKED TO BE AS SHORT AND POIGNANT AS POSSIBLE so that men who don't read much might take a shot at it because of its brevity. Below are five blog posts I wrote on the Purity Pursuit website. I rewrote all my material that is included in this book and didn't cut and paste off the blog; however, these five blog posts cover subjects that didn't make the book and need to be read. Like the five smooth stones of David, they're giant killers.

GO TO WWW.PURITYPURSUIT.COM AND SEARCH THESE TITLES:

1. Jesus Wept
2. Manhood
3. Acceptance
4. God Designed Pleasure
5. Holiday Sex

Made in the USA
Charleston, SC
05 March 2014